Your Local Area
SCHOOL

Ruth Thomson

Photography by Neil Thomson

WAYLAND

First published in 2010 by Wayland

Copyright © Wayland 2010

Wayland
338 Euston Road
London NW1 3BH

Wayland Australia
Hachette Children's Books
Level 17/207 Kent Street
Sydney NSW 2000

Editor: Nicola Edwards
Designer: Edward Kinsey
Design Manager: Paul Cherrill

British Library Cataloguing in Publication Data

Thomson, Ruth, 1949-
Your local area.
Schools.
1. Schools--Juvenile literature.
I. Title
371-dc22

ISBN: 978 0 7502 6088 6

The author would like to thank the following schools and individuals for their participation as well as their generosity in sharing ideas for this book: Laura Wynne at Argyle School, Camden, London: pages 2, 6cl, 6bl, 8tr, 10, 12cl, 12bl, 14bl, 15, 16tr, 18bl, 18tr, 18cr, 19cr, 19bl, 19br, 20tr, 21bl, 24t, 25tr, 25bl, 26tl, 26tr, 27tl, 27tc, 27tr, 28t, 29cr, 29bl, 29bc; Graham Nagel-Smith and Angus Reid at Morgan's Vale and Woodfalls Primary School, Morgan's Vale, Redlynch, Salisbury: pages 3, 5bl, 5br, 11br, 12-13, 14tr, 14br, 16b, 17, 20cl, 20bl, 20br, 21tl, 21br, 22, 23, 24bl, 25tl, 25br, 26cl, 26cr, 26br, 27 br, 28 tl; Alison Coe and Zoe Girling at Stanwick Primary School Stanwick, near Wellingborough: pages 6cr, 7, 11bl, 16c, 18cl, 18br, 19tl 19tr, 19cl, 29cr.

ISBN: 978 0 7502 6088 6

Printed in China

Wayland is a division of Hachette Children's Books, an Hachette UK Company.
www.hachette.co.uk

Free downloadable material is available to complement the activities in the Your Local Area series, including worksheets, templates for charts and photographic identification charts. For more information go to:
www.waylandbooks.co.uk/yourlocalarea
<http://www.waylandbooks.co.uk/yourlocalarea>

Contents

Schools old and new

School buildings vary in shape and size. They are all surrounded by space where children can play in breaks. In big towns and cities, many children go to large schools that the Victorians built. These have two or more floors and high brick walls around the playground.

 Why were Victorian schools built with such large windows?

SIGN OF THE PAST

In the past, boys and girls were taught separately, on different floors. They had separate playgrounds, as well, divided by a wall.

A stone plaque shows when a school was built.

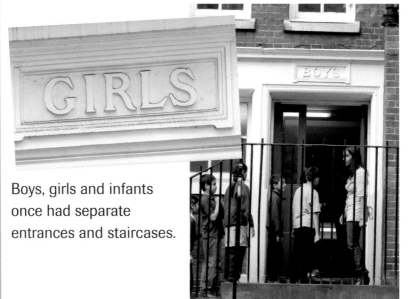

Boys, girls and infants once had separate entrances and staircases.

The chimneys were for the coal stoves that heated classrooms in winter.

Modern schools are usually built on only one floor. They usually have several doors out on to the playground. Many new schools, like this one, are landscaped with shrubs and flowerbeds and have playground equipment. Some village schools, like this one below, were once churches.

Where is your school?

There are schools wherever children live – in cities, towns or villages. Schools can be on a busy road near shops and businesses or on a quiet road surrounded by homes. Some are in the centre of a village.

What can you see through the windows of your school? Paint your favourite view.

A local look

Explore the roads around your school.
★ **Are there homes nearby?**
★ **What shops and services are there?**
★ **Is there a bus stop, canal or railway line nearby?**
★ **What landmark is nearest your school?**
★ **Mark your findings on a map.**

the war memorial

★ **Compare your findings with those of this village school. What is the same? What is different?**

the church

the graveyard

the village post office and café

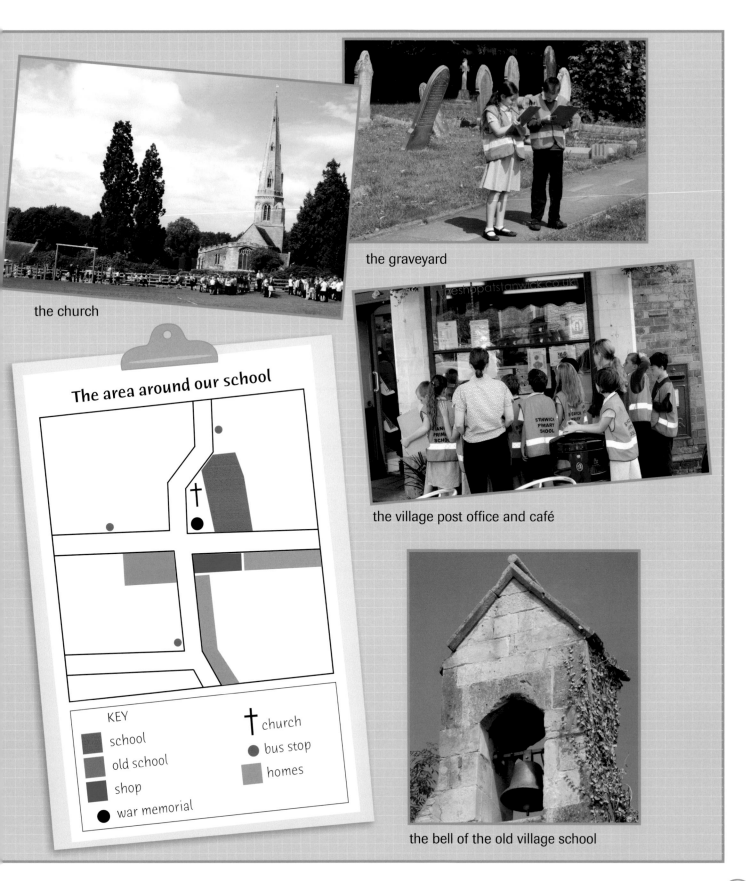

The area around our school

KEY
school
old school
shop
⚫ war memorial
✝ church
● bus stop
homes

the bell of the old village school

The route to school

Children come to school in different ways. They walk or cycle, come by car or take a bus.

Usually, they follow the same route, passing the same places and crossing the same roads every day.

? How do you travel to school?
What landmarks do you pass on the journey?

open space

housing

shops

A local look

★ Can you describe your route to school to a partner? Name the main roads and places you pass on the way.

★ Draw a map of your route to school or mark the route on a map of your local area.

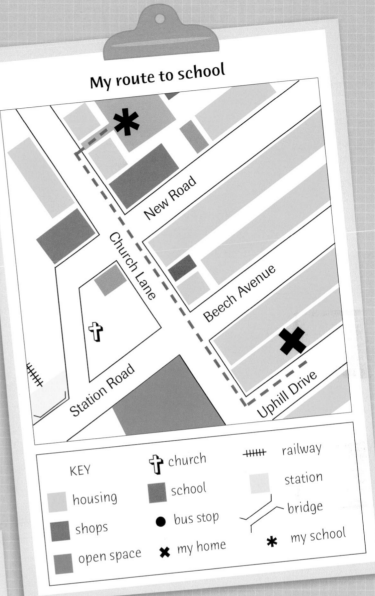

My route to school

KEY
✝ church
housing
▭ school
● bus stop
✖ my home
shops
open space
╫ railway
▭ station
⌐ bridge
✳ my school

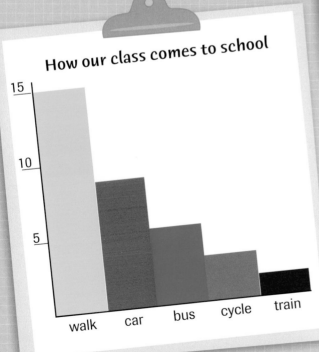

How our class comes to school

15
10
5

walk   car   bus   cycle   train

★ Discover who lives nearest and who lives furthest from your school.

★ Find out how your class comes to school and make a chart of your results.

★ Do children who live near school use the same method of transport as those who live further away?

9

Safe roads near school

The road outside schools are made safe for children. Road signs and yellow SCHOOL KEEP CLEAR road markings tell drivers they cannot stop outside the school gates. A metal barrier on the pavement stops children from running into the road.

Why are cars not allowed to stop outside school gates?

A local look

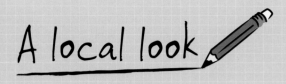

Take a walk along the road outside your school.

Humped zebra crossing

★ **What road signs and markings warn drivers that they are nearing a school?**

zebra crossing

★ **Are there any special pedestrian crossings, such as zebra, pelican or patrolled crossings?**
★ **Make a map of the roads around your school. Mark on it all the road signs, markings and crossings.**

Rooms at school

All schools, whatever their shape or size, have rooms with similar uses. The biggest room is the hall where the whole school can meet.

There are classrooms, offices, storerooms, toilets and a kitchen. Schools may also have a library, a quiet room, an IT room, a music room and an art room.

What rooms does your school have?

A local look

★ Look at this plan of a small school.
★ Why are the offices near the entrance and the kitchen near the hall?
★ Why are the classrooms grouped together and the toilets, as well?

classroom

head teacher's office

cloakroom

My school

playground entrance

back entrance

main entrance

KEY
- hall
- classroom
- kitchen
- library
- offices
- storeroom
- staff room
- toilets
- quiet room

This is where we have assemblies in the morning, do gym and have lunch. Sometimes we perform plays and concerts here as well.

The staff drink coffee here.

★ **Photocopy or draw a plan of your school. Write a guide to show visitors around, describing the main rooms.**
★ **Take photographs of the rooms to illustrate your guide.**

Who works at a school?

All sorts of people work in a school. The head teacher is in charge. Teachers and teaching assistants help children learn. Sometimes, parents and other volunteers come to help children too. The school site manager, cleaners and a gardener make sure the school buildings and grounds are kept clean.

A local look

teacher

★ **Make a list of all the people who work at your school. Include the teachers and assistants who work there all day and people who come in at particular times of day, such as cooks and cleaners.**

cleaner

? What do people in the front office do?

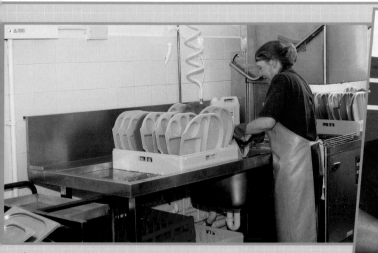

cooks

school site manager

gardener

★ **Write a list of questions you would like to ask people.**

Questions

- What do you do in your job?
- How long have you been doing it?
- What do you like about it?
- Is there anything you dislike?

★ **Use the answers to write a description of each person's job.**
★ **Put them together to make a book called *People who work at my school.***

The school grounds

Most schools in built-up areas of big towns and cities have small grounds with hard playing surfaces. In suburbs, villages and the country, there is space for schools to have larger grounds, often with a field and trees.

 Where can you find these surfaces in your grounds? Why have they been used in each particular place?

| decking | rubber | asphalt | paving | grass | bark chip |

A local look

Look at this plan of a school's grounds.
★ Which parts are used in fine weather and which might be used in bad weather?

★ How are the grounds shielded from the road?
★ Why do Reception children have their own play area?

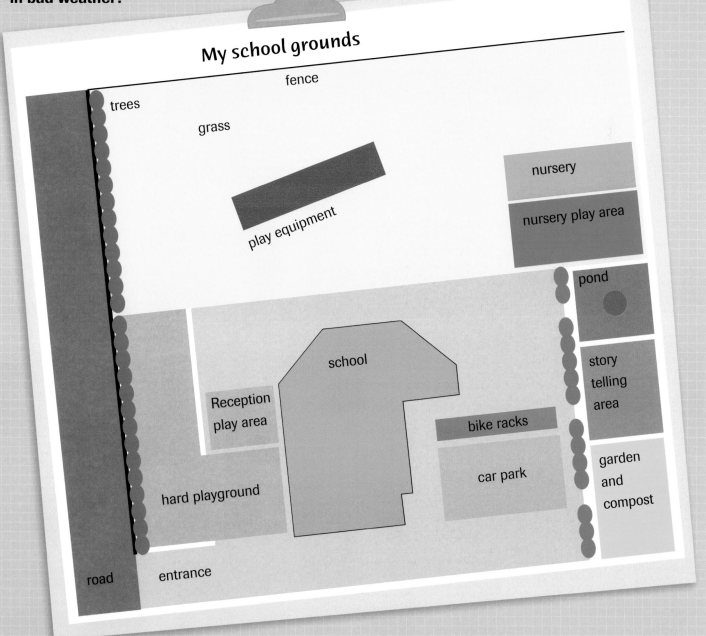

My school grounds

fence

trees

grass

play equipment

nursery

nursery play area

pond

school

Reception play area

story telling area

bike racks

car park

garden and compost

hard playground

road   entrance

★ Draw a plan of your school grounds and buildings. Mark the spaces used for different activities.

★ Tick the spots that you like best.
★ Put a cross on the areas you dislike. Think about why you feel the way you do.

Playtime

The playground is a space which children have to share for different activities. Some playgrounds have games already marked out, a space for running around and a quiet area.

? How have these pieces of equipment been designed so that lots of children can use them at the same time?

A local look

★ **Do a survey to find out what are the most popular games and activities at playtime.**

★ **What ball games do children like playing the most?**

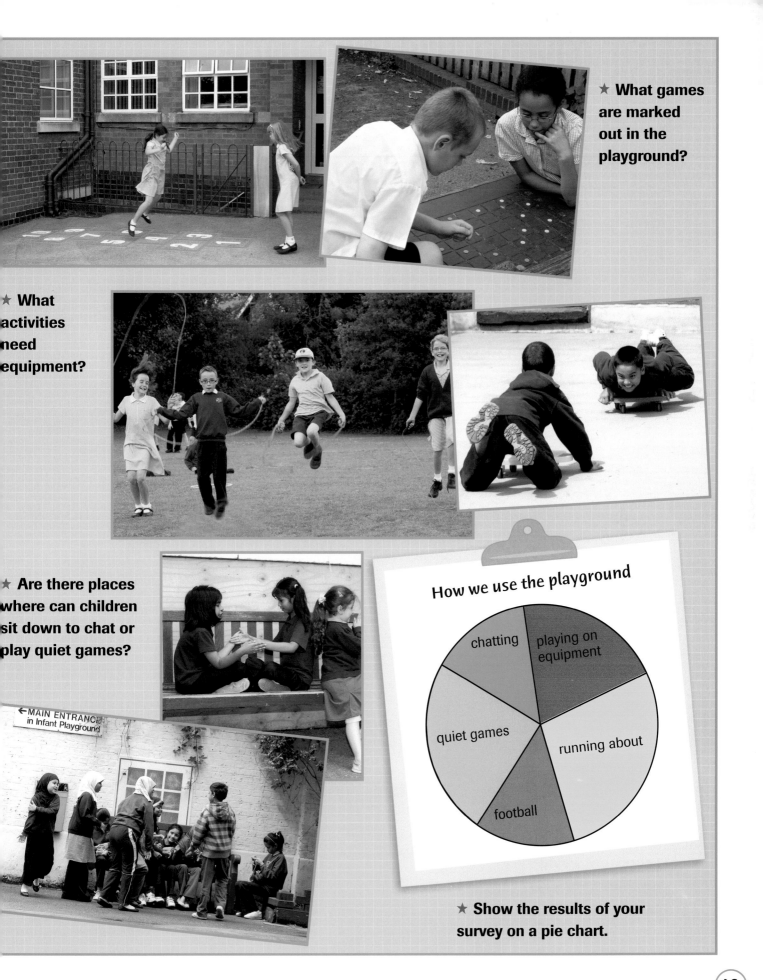

★ **What games are marked out in the playground?**

★ **What activities need equipment?**

★ **Are there places where can children sit down to chat or play quiet games?**

←MAIN ENTRANCE
in Infant Playground

How we use the playground

chatting

playing on equipment

quiet games

running about

football

★ **Show the results of your survey on a pie chart.**

Improving the grounds

Schools make their grounds more cheerful and interesting with extra decoration and furniture. Some paint blank walls or make outdoor artworks.

Many put baskets and containers of colourful flowers in bare corners. Others build wet weather shelters or fit new playground equipment.

Outdoor spaces provide a good place to meet, talk, listen and learn outside the classroom.

A local carpenter made this giant chair, so children at this school could listen to stories outdoors. He made a table where children meet if they have problems at playtime.

What new piece of furniture would you choose for your school grounds?

A local look

Discuss ways in which you could help improve your school grounds.

★ Could you hold a competition to design a mosaic for a blank brick wall?

★ Could you design a weaving, reusing old plastic bags to hide a wire netting fence?

★ Could you design a mural for a bare wall or even turn it into a climbing wall, as this school has done?

★ Could you create outdoor sculptures from junk materials?

School gardens

Another way schools improve their grounds is by planting flowers and vegetables in pots and beds.

This school built wooden beds. In spring, children filled them with compost and soil and planted seeds. By summer, the plants had grown tall.

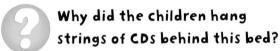
Why did the children hang strings of CDs behind this bed?

The children take turns to plant new flowers, water the plants, weed the beds and empty the weeds into the compost heap.

A local look

★ Think of good ways to attract wildlife.

★ Hang up a bird feeder and nesting materials in quiet spots.

★ Could you persuade your school to build a pond? Then you can study water plants and pondlife all year round.

★ Build a minibeast hotel, using wooden pallets, airbricks, clay tiles and pots. Make sure each layer is stable before you add the next one.

★ Fill the gaps with bamboo, twigs and grass, so minibeasts have somewhere safe to hide.

Reducing rubbish

Schools produce a lot of rubbish. Some of it, such as paper, aluminium cans, plastic bottles and food waste can be recycled. In many schools, children help collect and sort the rubbish for recycling. They also make sure the school is kept clean by putting litter in rubbish bins.

? Where do people drop rubbish at your school? Where are the litter bins? Which spots need a bin?

A local look

At your school council, discuss ways that children could help reduce rubbish.

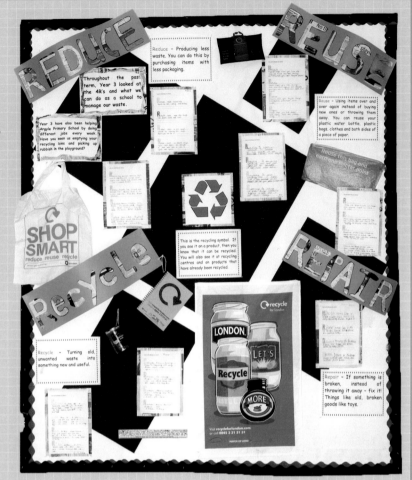

★ Could you keep food waste separate and compost it?
★ Make a chart showing what you can and cannot compost.

★ Could you make a display encouraging everyone at school to reduce, reuse, recycle and repair?

★ Could you take turns picking up litter?

★ Try this experiment. Bury a metal can, a plastic bottle and bag, a glass bottle, some paper and fruit skins.
★ Make some labelled markers for them.
★ Dig them up a year later and see how well they have rotted away.

Saving resources

Schools are finding ways to save resources and make their environment more sustainable.

Schools that have a suitable space install a water butt to harvest rainwater from the roof.

? How is harvested rainwater used at this school?

Cardboard reuse or Recycle

Empty and washed plastic milk bottles

Empty 2 litre fizzy drink bottles

Many classes recycle paper and cardboard. Some schools encourage children and parents to bring in plastic bottles and lids, flower pots, used wrapping paper and other unwanted things. These are used instead of new materials for art and science projects, like this friendship tree.

At the end of each day, a team of Power Rangers go round this school. They switch off any lights and electrical equipment that have been left on.

The Power Rangers award points to each class for using electricity sensibly.

Power ranger points
0 points = all appliances were left on
1 point = some were turned off
2 points = all were turned off

They mark the points on a weekly chart. At the end of term, they give a prize to the class with most points.

Power ranger weekly class points						
Class	Monday	Tuesday	Wednesday	Thursday	Friday	Total
Reception	1	1				
Year 1	2	1				
Year 2	2	2				
Year 3	1	1				
Year 4	2	1				
Year 5	1	1				
Year 6	2	2				

Winning class of the week:

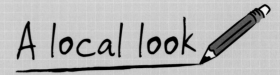

A local look

Discuss ways that your school could help save resources.

You can save water by making sure you turn off taps properly.

You can refill reusable plastic bottles rather than buying new drinks in cartons or bottles.

You could organise regular old clothes collections for a charity.

More things to do

Where do the families of children at your school come from?

★ **Make a welcome poster using either a map of the UK showing relevant towns and villages, or of the world showing relevant countries and flags.**

★ **Find out how to write 'Welcome' in other languages. Add these words to your poster.**

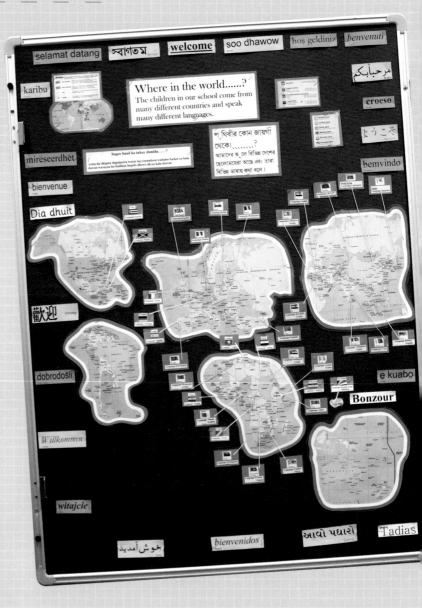

Children must be safe at school. Many schools lock doors and gates once children have arrived. Visitors must ring a bell to be let in.

★ **What happens when visitors come to your school?**

A fire at school would be dangerous. Every school has fire alarms, fire exits and fire extinguishers in case of an emergency.

★ **Look around your school to find out where these are.**

★ **What must you do if the fire alarm rings?**

Take photographs or draw sketches of things and places all round your school and its grounds.

★ Where feels bright and welcoming?

★ Where is tidy and organised?

★ Which places are quiet? Which are often noisy?

★ Are there any spots which look messy or feel neglected? What would you suggest to improve them?

bright fencing

painted compost bin

signed trays in a classroom

tidy shelves for lunchboxes

comfortable library

decorated water fountains

colourful tiles on a staircase

organised cloakroom

Glossary

assembly a time when people come together as a group

barrier a fence used to stop people getting past

chimney a passage above a fire where smoke can escape outdoors

coal a hard black rock made of carbon that is mined from underground and burned as fuel

fire extinguisher a metal container with foam or chemical inside that people can spray on a fire to put it out

grounds the land that surrounds a building

junk unwanted or useless things

landmark a place, often a building, that helps you know where you are, because it is easy to see

litter rubbish, such as drinks cans or food wrappers, which people drop on to the ground

mosaic a design formed by closely fitting together small pieces of coloured tiles or glass

mural a picture painted directly on to a wall

outskirts the outer areas of a town or city

pallet a wooden platform on which things are stacked, so they can be moved by a fork-lift truck

pelican crossing a crossing where people press a button to change traffic lights to red, so that they can cross a busy road

plaque a stone or metal plate fixed to a wall or building with writing on it. It usually marks a specific event or person.

recycle to process waste materials to turn them back into something useful

route a way of getting somewhere

suburb an area of houses and flats on the outer edges of towns and cities

surface the top layer of something

Victorian the time when Queen Victoria ruled Britain – from 1837 to 1901

war memorial something put up to remember people who died in a war

zebra crossing a pedestrian crossing with black and white road markings and a flashing orange light, called a Belisha Beacon, on the pavement at either side

?Talking points

The questions in the book encourage close observation of the pictures and provide talking points for discussion.

Pages 4-5
• Victorian schools offer clues about schooling in the past. The words BOYS, GIRLS and INFANTS are often still marked above the entrances. There may be a separate building once used for cookery or manual training workshops. Huge windows let in as much light as possible at a time when gaslamps were in use for lighting. The hard surfaced playground was used for drill, exercise where children bent, stretched and jumped in time to teachers' orders.
• Children could find out about the history of their own school, using local archives. The school may also have its own records and photographs children could look at.

Pages 6-7
• Some schools are near a church. Others may be set in areas of housing. Local features or landmarks might include a nearby park, shopping parade, town hall or library. As well as painting, children could photograph local places of interest. They could make a guide to their local area and incorporate these pictures.

Pages 8-9
• Children could discuss the drawbacks and benefits of travelling to school using different forms of transport. Discuss schemes, such as 'a walking bus' that might be introduced to save car or bus journeys and give children some regular exercise.

Pages 10-11
• Looking at how school road signs and markings promote safety could lead to a wider discussion about how and where to cross roads safely, including how to use crossings, such as a zebra or pelican crossing. See the website: http://talesoftheroad.direct.gov.uk/stop-look-listen.php
• Ask children to look at other road signs that control speed or keep pedestrians and bikes safe from traffic.

Pages 12-13
• Children could record all the places they go in school during a day or a week. Where do they spend most of their time? Is there any room they never go to? If not, why not?
• Children could record the movement of pupils through the school at different times of day. When are the corridors busiest? When does the whole school get together? Are there any areas that are always quiet?

Pages 14-15
• The people in the front office welcome visitors, answer phone calls, send out letters and do other office work to make sure the school runs efficiently.

Pages 16-17
• Ask children to consider why their grounds are laid out as they are. Nursery and reception children have their own areas, with water, sand and other equipment, where they can play all day long, not just at playtime. The fencing makes sure children do not wander off on their own.
• Discuss the uses of different play surfaces and how play activities change throughout the year. Grass is ideal in fine weather, but can turn muddy in the rain. Rubber provides a soft landing if children fall off equipment. Hard surfaces are good for running and jumping games, such as hopscotch. Decking is a useful surface around a pond.

Pages 18-19
• The two examples shown have different elements for climbing, balancing, swinging and hanging, which several children can use at the same time. Children might like to design their own playground equipment or obstacle course.
• Ask children to compile some playground rules, which make the playground a safe and fair place for everyone.

Pages 20-21
• Canvass children's opinions about improvements they would like to see. Discuss both small-scale improvements that could be effected quickly and easily, such as putting out hanging baskets or plant pots or painting litter or compost bins, and longer-term ones, such as making murals, weavings or creating outdoor classrooms, sensory or musical gardens. Think about different pieces of furniture, as well.

Pages 22-23
• The CDs move and shimmer to scare away birds.
• There are lots of ideas for creating wildlife gardens at Learning Through Landscapes: http://ltl.org.uk.

Pages 24-25
• Recycle now has information, activities and bin stickers and downloadable posters about recycling and school composting at http://recycle.now.com/schools/index.html
• Children can survey the playground to find areas where litter is always dropped. They could paint a litter bin to make it stand out as a playground feature.

Pages 26-27
• Recycling initiatives could involve families and even the wider community – asking for otherwise unwanted materials.
• Consider adopting the idea of Power Rangers and giving a 'green' prize to the best class.
• Ask children to produce posters that could be put up in relevant spots reminding them to save resources.
• A water butt is used to harvest rainwater from the roof.

Index